Voices from Vickers

The Workers' Story

Compiled by Phil Kitchen

Tyne Bridge Publishing

Acknowledgements:

Many thanks to Andrea Armstrong of Vickers Defence Systems and Fred Millican of West Newcastle Local Studies for their help with picture research and glossary.

Edited by Anna Flowers and Vanessa Histon, Tyne Bridge Publishing. Research and introduction by Ken Smith.

Photographs are copyright of Newcastle Libraries & Information Service unless otherwise indicated.

The views expressed in this book are entirely personal to the contributors and in no way reflect the opinions of Newcastle City Council.

Published by
City of Newcastle upon Tyne
Education & Libraries Directorate
Newcastle Libraries & Information Service
Tyne Bridge Publishing
2001

ISBN: 1 85795 1115

Printed by statexcolourprint, Newcastle upon Tyne

Front cover: the VSG section at the end of World War II.
Back cover: A Doxford crankshaft.

More books on the industrial history of Tyneside from Tyne Bridge Publishing:

Down Elswick Slipways: Armstrong's Ships and People 1884-1918, Dick Keys and Ken Smith, £5.99.

Emperor of Industry: Lord Armstrong of Cragside, Ken Smith, £2.50.

From Walker to the World: Charles Mitchell's Low Walker Shipyard, Dick Keys and Ken Smith, £4.99.

Mauretania: Pride of the Tyne, Ken Smith, £4.99.

On the Waterfront: An Historical Tour of Newcastle's Quayside, Ian Ayris and Patricia Sheldon, £6.99.

Swan Hunter: the Pride and the Tears, Ken Smith, £5.99.

Turbinia: The Story of Charles parsons and his Ocean Greyhound, Ken Smith, £4.99.

Water Under the Bridges: Newcastle's 20th Century, various authors, introduced by Professor Norman McCord, £9.99.

A free catalogue is available from
Tyne Bridge Publishing
City Library
Princess Square
Newcastle upon Tyne
NE99 1DX

Tel: 0191 2774174
Fax: 0191 2774137

see our website for the latest information:
www.newcastle.gov.uk/tynebridgepublishing

Preface

1997 was the 150th anniversary of the opening of Armstrong's factory, the birth of a giant operation. The company, through various incarnations as Armstrong's, Armstrong Whitworth, Vickers-Armstrongs and finally Vickers, has over the years employed vast numbers of Tynesiders and made numerous products in its two factories at Elswick and Scotswood. The history of the company illustrates the massive changes which have taken place in manufacturing and industry in the North-East over the last 150 years.

In the anniversary year I was involved in developing new educational activity for Newcastle's Adult Basic Education Service. Des Walton of West Newcastle Local Studies suggested a project involving workers and ex-workers of Vickers. I was immediately enthusiastic about the idea.

Alma Wheeler, who had worked for many years in Vickers Personnel Department, and Tommy Spence, Union Convenor, gave me invaluable help in contacting workers whose stories and reminiscences covered over 70 years.

Contributions were made by George Carr, James Routledge, Neville and Ethel Armstrong, Alma Wheeler, Alan Evans, William Wilson, John Daglish, William Waggott, William Bell, William Jeffries, John Thompson, Tommy Spence, John Tones, Edward Mullin, Frank Kay, Eric Shields, Jack Rowell, Rebecca Watson, J.J. Kearns, Henry Hall, Lisa Mordue, Dorothy Harm and Pat Marvell.

Particular thanks to Alma Wheeler, Tommy Spence, William Jeffries, Des Walton and Fred Millican for their help in the organisation of the project, and to Ken Smith for writing such an informative introduction.

Phil Kitchen, 2001

Contents

Home time. The subway entrance to Elswick Works c.late 1940s. Workers are running for the tram at the end of shift. The entrance to 28 Shop is bottom left, and No. 4 Forge is to the right.

Vickers – The Great North Arms Maker

In 1847 lawyer William Armstrong founded the Elswick Works on the banks of the Tyne in the West End of Newcastle to manufacture his invention, the hydraulic crane. His business venture was to grow into one of the world's greatest armaments and shipbuilding empires and become Newcastle's largest employer.

The hydraulic crane, ideal for railways and docks, and other hydraulic machinery such as dock gates were among the early products of the Elswick Works. Later, however, spurred by problems experienced with artillery during the Crimean War, Armstrong branched out into gun-making. His breech-loading field gun, which was accurate and mobile, was to be adopted by the British government. Armstrong was knighted for his invention of this gun, but it eventually fell out of official favour, largely due to the conservatism of British Army officers.

However, the company was by no means daunted by this development. Elswick began manufacturing naval guns and this led to a deal with shipbuilder Charles Mitchell who owned a yard at Low Walker in Newcastle's East End. It was decided that Low Walker would build the warships and Elswick equip them with guns. This proved a highly successful Tyneside partnership.

However, in order to meet potential demand it was eventually decided that a second shipyard should be opened, this time at the Elswick Works.

The new yard was set up in 1884 and launched its first ship, the Austro-Hungarian torpedo-cruiser *Panther*, the following year. Meanwhile, Armstrong and Mitchell's businesses had merged and it was agreed that Elswick should concentrate mainly on warships and Low Walker on merchant vessels.

Over more than 30 years the Elswick Shipyard turned out warships for many nations, including Japan, China, Chile,

Vickers

Elswick Works, 1847.

Argentina, and Brazil as well as Britain. The yard was particularly noted for its fast, protected cruisers. Elswick ships and guns helped Admiral Togo of Japan win the Battle of Tsushima against the Russians in 1905.

The Elswick Works developed into one of the world's largest arsenals, producing numerous guns as well as hydraulic gun carriages and mountings. Armstrong's also began to manufacture shells, shot and fuses and opened a works at Scotswood for this purpose.

As well as the hydraulic crane, Elswick's products included the machinery and iron superstucture of Newcastle's Swing Bridge, completed in 1876. This replaced an 18th century bridge with low, narrow arches, which was a barrier to large ships. The Swing Bridge enabled Elswick-built vessels to pass down river to the sea. In addition, the company constructed the opening machinery for London's Tower Bridge, completed in the 1890s.

All these developments led to an enormous increase in the workforce. Elswick provided employment for many people on Tyneside. Housing for the workers sprang up throughout Newcastle's West End. Indeed, the development of the West End as an urban area can in large measure be attributed to the work provided by Armstrong's factories.

A significant development came in 1897 when Armstrong's amalgamated with Sir Joseph Whitworth's Manchester-based armaments business, and was renamed Armstrong, Whitworth.

By 1900 Elswick was employing many thousands of people, a great number of them living close to the works in the city's West End. In the ordance department guns were produced ranging from 110-ton breech-loaders to small machine guns. The works also featured workshops (shops) in which huge steel mountings were made to carry the heaviest

Armament production at one of the Armstrong, Whitworth factories during World War I. Twenty-one thousand women were employed.

Vickers

armour-piercing guns as well as tiny carriages for small seven-pounder weapons.

Despite its success in the field of gun production, Armstrong's continued to turn out non-military products. By 1906, for example, it had set up a motor car works at Scotswood. The Low Walker Shipyard built many merchant vessels, gaining a good reputation for its pioneering oil tankers.

In 1912-13 Armstrong's opened a new shipbuilding base, the Naval Yard at Walker, Newcastle. Its first vessel was the battleship HMS *Malaya*. This yard was eventually to replace the one at Elswick.

During the First World War the company made an immense contribution to Britain's efforts when it manufactured 13,000 guns, over 14 million shells and around 100 pioneering tanks. Women workers from Tyneside proved their worth in the factories.

Warships continued to be launched for Britain's fleet throughout the conflict. The firm also expanded into aircraft production, setting up a biplane factory on the edge of the Duke's Moor, Gosforth, Newcastle, to supply Britain's emerging airforce. Following the war, the company's output included locomotives. These were built at Scotswood.

In 1927-1928 came a highly significant development when most of the company's business interests were merged with those of Vickers to form Vickers-Armstrongs Ltd. The new company was to go from strength to strength.

The advent of the Second World War in 1939 saw Vickers-Armstrongs at the forefront of armaments manufacture. In 1939 Elswick employed more than 12,000 people and Scotswood over 6,000.

Women workers from Tyneside, as well as men, again proved vital. The company undoubtedly played a major role in the victory of the Allies, with Elswick and Scotswood becoming a hub of the war effort. In addition, the Walker Naval Yard launched numerous vessels, including the battleship HMS *King George V*. From 1934 Elswick was engaged on rearmament work, with tanks, armoured cars, and track vehicles featuring among its many products. During the war its enormously varied output of Elswick and Scotswood included Infantry (Valentine) Tanks, Light Tanks, Cruiser Tanks, guns and turrets for warships, anti-aircraft guns, Howitzers and shells. Vital parts for RAF aircraft undercarriages and gun turrets were only manufactured at Elswick and Scotswood.

After the war Vickers-Armstrongs continued to produce tanks as well as ships. For a while even tractors and printing presses were made at Elswick and Scotswwod. By the 1950s the Elswick and Scotswood works comprised 70 acres of engineering shops, machine shops and foundries. Steel and non-ferrous forgings and castings were among the company's most important post-war products. Car components were also manufactured. In 1963 Elswick employed 5,700 people and Scotswood 1,300. Two years later, in 1965, Vickers-Armstrongs' business was absorbed into Vickers Ltd. In 1982 Vickers Defence Systems, a division of Vickers Plc, opened its new Armstrong Works, on the site of the old Scotswood Works, for the production of tanks. In the same year the historic Elswick Works closed. Elswick had concentrated mainly on the production of tanks during its last years and the civilian, commercial side of the business, including the foundries, had ceased operation.

The decline in the numbers of people employed following the Second World War reflected the general decline in British heavy industry. The world wars had been the high point both in terms of activity and numbers on the payroll.

The memories of people who worked at Elswick and Scotswood are featured in the following pages. More vivid than any conventional historical account, their experiences tell a colourful and fascinating human story.

Ken Smith

Learning to be the Workers – the Apprentices

For many boys, getting an apprenticeship was an important first step on the road to job security. You learned a trade and in many cases you had a job for life in one of the manufacturing centres on Tyneside, or in the armed forces. Life could be tough for the apprentices – long hours at work followed by night school. Most felt they got good training, though some were resentful of being used as cheap labour. In some periods apprentices were laid off when they had served their time.

GETTING A START

Getting an apprenticeship was important. It was like going to university now. It was a job for life, though it was traditional to get rid of apprentices when they came out of their time. They were expected to get a still better job with another firm or in the forces (particularly the Navy on Tyneside) – to get more experience. At Vickers, priority was given to relatives of employees and footballers.

John Tones

THE APPRENTICE'S LIFE

After the end of the First World War the hours were reduced to 47 hours per week, and apprenticeships were reduced to five years. An agreement was signed with the parent or guardian and the employer to complete a five year apprenticeship. The majority of boys were to serve their time as fitters and turners, but other boys were apprenticed as coppersmiths, blacksmiths, electricians and boilermakers. There was also an intake of boys as machine hands who were not indentured. They worked milling, drilling, slotting, grinding and capstan machines … after a few years many of them became highly skilled operators.

In the late Twenties and Thirties if an apprentice attended night schools and passed the Ordinary National Certificate, he could augment his wages by taking the yearly examination and passing in three subjects. The reward was one shilling for sitting and fourpence for passing each subject. Two shillings on his wages! Then at the age of 18, if his foreman thought he was worth it, he could receive two shillings class money or efficiency money on his weekly wage. This increased to three shillings and sixpence in his last years. On completion of his apprenticeship he would receive a sum of about £9 which was made up over the five years by a weekly deduction of threepence from his wages and sixpence from the employer. This money was supposed to help the apprentice to buy tools when he became a journeyman. If during his five years he had been absent, he had to work up that time which was called 'Black Time'.

Alan Evans

1930S APPRENTICE

Having gone to a technical school I was able to go straight on to a lathe, turning test pieces in the Test Room. My immediate thoughts that first morning were what a long time I had been at work! I was jolted back to reality when I saw the office staff arriving at 8.45am and realised it was to be a long day – indeed a long week in prospect. This of course included Saturday mornings when I would probably have been playing for the school football team.

After a few months, on approaching my 16th birthday, I was transferred to the Toolroom. There we certainly learned what accuracy and measured tolerance were about. The toolmakers, when they talked about tenths, it was not of an inch but tenths of a thou. I thought I would never be able to acquire their skill on the machines or on the bench. I did however realise, despite their undoubted skills as toolmakers, that some of them were compulsive liars who had all run a hundred yards in ten seconds. From out of the workshop windows we had marvellous views right up the Tyne Valley and the rambling workshops which had probably been created in Armstrong's time.

With the rearmament programme accelerating, many of the workshops were being re-built. We in the toolroom had a real bird's eye view of the demolition and rebuilding of 29 Shop, the hub of Elswick Works. The most spectacular part was the yard locomotive pulling a main stanchion out, for the roof structure to collapse. The amazing part was that men carried out work in the safer parts of the shop whilst this was all taking

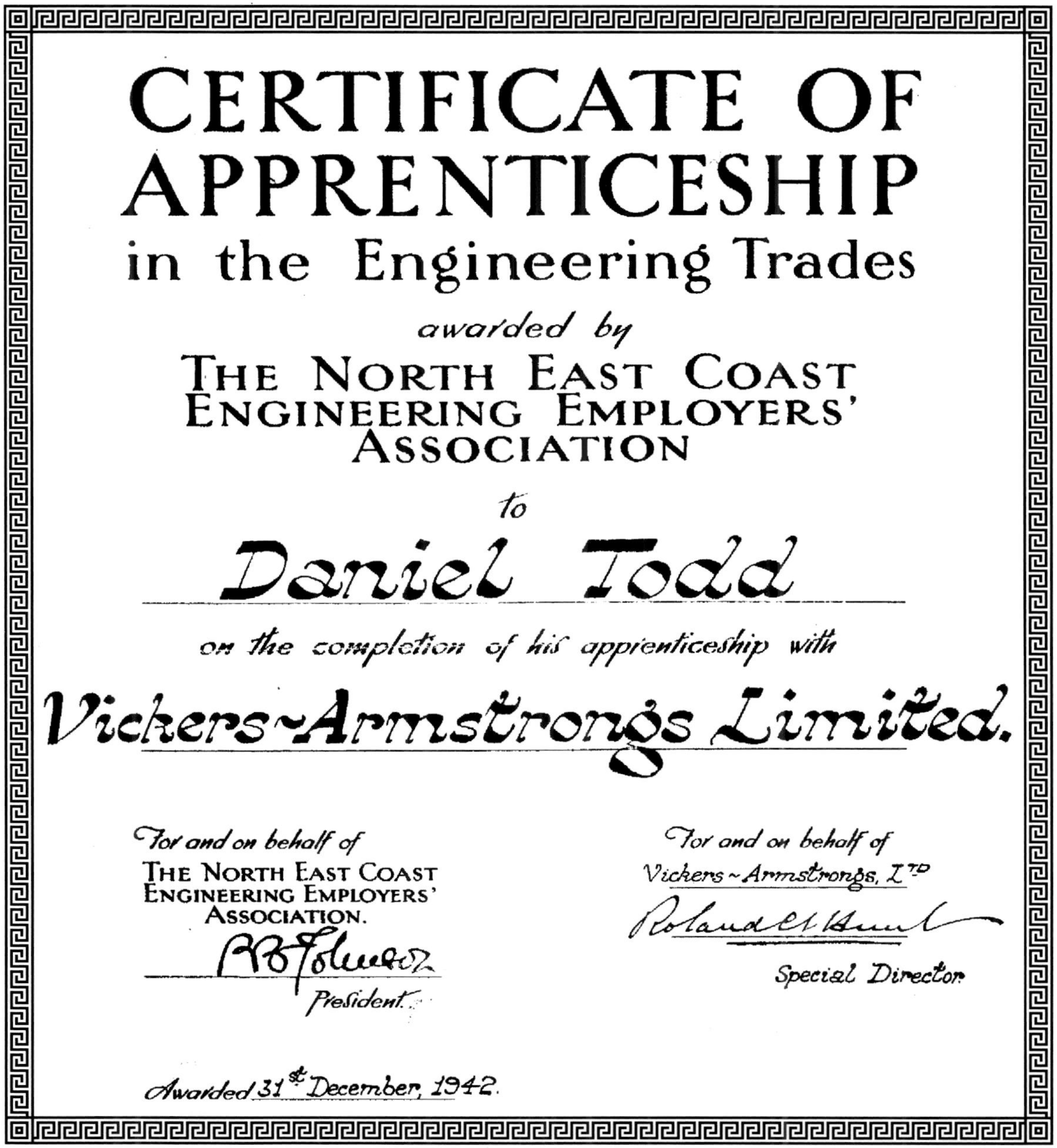

CERTIFICATE OF APPRENTICESHIP
in the Engineering Trades

awarded by

THE NORTH EAST COAST ENGINEERING EMPLOYERS' ASSOCIATION

to

Daniel Todd

on the completion of his apprenticeship with

Vickers~Armstrongs Limited.

For and on behalf of
THE NORTH EAST COAST ENGINEERING EMPLOYERS' ASSOCIATION.

President.

For and on behalf of
Vickers~Armstrongs, LTD

Special Director

Awarded 31st December, 1942.

place. Out of the east windows we were able to witness the building of 22 Shop which was to house all the breech mechanism work and gun sights. Before the work could take place a large brick chimney had to be felled and we were quite convinced it would crash through the Toolroom roof. However with pinpoint accuracy it collapsed fifty yards short.

In the summer dinner hours we would sit out on the jetty watching the river traffic and often witness some wonderful feats of engineering. The large jib crane built by Armstrong would lift a complete 6 inch triple gun mounting out of the assembly pits through the roof of 24 Shop and lower it into the admiralty barge to be taken down to the Naval Yard or Swan Hunter's, there to be fitted into a City Class Cruiser. We saw trials in the river of probably the first amphibian tank. The construction laced with balsa wood would plough a few nautical feet up and down the river. Other interesting episodes were trials of quadruple deck mounted torpedo tubes. A wooden dummy torpedo was fired out into the river and then hauled back to the river side. Yes, life in the dinner hours on the jetty was very interesting.

Students of Rutherford Technical College photographed during a tour of Scotswood Works c.1930.

Other memories come flooding back, how you had to get used to going to work in the dark and coming home in the dark for at least three months of the year. The horrible icy winters when scores of men picked their way down St John's Road which joined into Edgeware Road forming what some old hands called the 'compound angle', treacherous underfoot. Then there was 'Curds and Cream' Road which was a continuation of the subway entrance to the works, it was supposed to be a public road but it was only used by the workforce. It was Vickers original Black Hole. On the walls of this dark tunnel was every conceivable electric cable, water pipes, gas pipes, asbestos wrapped heating pipes, a veritable snake-pit of pipes. I had cause to go along that entrance about forty years later, and it appeared to be just the same

The jetty at Elswick, with hydraulic crane and fitting and gun shops 6 7 and 11, April 1969, prior to demolition.

West Newcastle Local Studies (Jimmy Forsyth)

Originally the Mechanics' Institute, this building on Scotswood Road later became the Apprentices' Welfare Club. Beyond is the school, which later became the Schools Canteen. The Mechanics and Foresters Arms is in the distance.

GETTING A TRAINING

There was no formal training of apprentices, a boy would be given jobs to do and receive limited instruction from some journeyman or chargehand. His progress was watched and as he improved he was given a higher standard of work.

The apprentices' supervisor, a Captain Gillman, moved the apprentices onto different work round the factory. He was an ex-army Captain, of tall bird-like appearance, who always referred to his charges as 'the boys' – in a strong Irish accent. His office was in the old school library and canteen building which still retained its Dickensian Mechanics Institute furnishings and atmosphere. If an apprentice had attained reasonable standards at night school he could be moved into the drawing office – this was generally for the last two years of his apprenticeship. This job carried staff status and, of course, shorter hours and a fortnight's holiday every year.

T. Jones

though possibly with more cables and pipes.

One had to have sympathy for the progress men who had to chase work the whole length of that rambling factory. From Head Office, Brass foundry to Water Street at three different levels. If a pedometer had been put on their feet the mileage they covered would have been quite incredible. Their reception in different shops was far from cordial of course!

By the mid-thirties the toolroom was moved to another new shop – 36 – part of Vickers building programme. It was very open plan in the new shop. There were no hiding places now!

Alan Evans

THE PLUMBERS' HARVEST TIME

'I started serving my time in November 1933 and I found out later it was known as the 'Plumbers' Harvest time', because of all the trouble with frozen and burst pipes. It wasn't bad in the offices and canteens – they had coal-fired boilers in the basements … the bursts kept us going for a while.

27 Shop was dormant, so a plumber and I went in there to strip all unwanted pipes and make it safe for the builders so they could lay the concrete floor. They managed to keep warm by burning the tarry floor blocks. I think the idea was that when they got the floor laid they would transfer the machines from 29 Shop so they could pull it down and rebuild. After laying the

machines in 27 Shop they introduced girl and woman operators to the capstan machines, which made more work, building cloakrooms and toilets, and so increased the staff on maintenance.

I was sent to work with a plumber in 33 Shop where we had to line wood tanks with lead for pickling purposes. This section also covered the fuse and cartridge [section] which was 39c. I had never seen so many machines with women operators and the machines were all belt operated. At the west end they had all the gauging benches. Then it got so busy they had to build a bridge across to the top floor of the main store shop and transfer the gauges so they could move machines. 39B was an extension of 33 when I first went in. There were only about 20 women working. They were welders and made floats for fishing nets. It wasn't long before they took over the rest of the shop for turning shell cases and benches for gauging the cases. The fuse and cartridge [section] didn't stop there. They had machines put into 60 Shop and, after taking over Scotswood works, machines and everything necessary were assembled. It also made more work for plumbers, new toilets and cloakrooms were needed.

G. Carr

Making floats for fishing boats in 33 Shop.

THE APPRENTICE PLATER

I started work at Vickers Elswick works in June 1930 and retired after 49 continuous years in September 1979.

I started in the plater's shop, 135, where they were building coal hoists for Leith and Barry docks. These are large structures for lifting the coal trucks to fill the ships, also Norfolk Spades which scooped the coal from the trucks. These were all riveted structures as welding was in its infancy. All the steel plates were sheared and the only burning equipment was a hand torch. The acetylene was made in a miniature gas holder, where a carbide was placed on a tray and water dripped on it to make acetylene.

We also had 23 angle smiths in the department making angle frames for 6 inch gun mountings for the Navy. These frames were all fire welded. A large vertical press bent the armour plate for the gun houses for the 6-inch mountings. We also manufactured housings for the torpedo tubes, also made two deck man-cages and large strips made of Duralumin, again all riveted, for the South African mines.

Leading up to the war, welding and burning made great strides and when the frames were made for the *King George V* and *Duke of York* [warships] these were all welded by arc welding and during the war all sorts of steel fabrications were made.

The conditions in the workshops were very basic. There was no heating as such: we were allowed to have coke braziers in the depot but we were not allowed to go near to them and they caused more dust than heat. So, combined with the angle smiths' fires, the atmosphere was not top class. The noise of armour plate and riveting was unbelievable as no one was issued with any protective equipment. No one seemed to protest … people were glad to have a job as there was no such thing as redundancy payment.

J.W. Rowell

OFFICE BOY TO DRAUGHTSMAN 1931-1938

A few days before my 14th birthday my father was told that the Marine Drawing Office of Armstrong, Whitworth required an office boy and if I could leave school early I could have the job. I started work when I was 14 years and four days old. It was a strange experience to go to work after school and family life. It was a five and a half day week, 8.30am - 12 noon and 1.00pm - 5.00pm and for this I received seven shillings and sixpence per week, less twopence, for the Sport Fund.

The staff of the Marine Drawing Office were as follows: Mr Mathews the Manager, Mr Kevney the Assistant Manager, Mr Harrison, the Chief Draughtsman. There were also about 30 draughtsmen, eight estimators including two ladies, and an office clerk – Mr Leslie – for whom I worked. My job was to run messages from the drawing office to other departments, to get a *Sporting Man* for Mr Thompson, every morning, and to go to Scotswood for anything the draughtsmen required.

The building which housed the Marine Drawing Office was long, glass-roofed and divided into two by a partition on the other side of which was the Locomotive Drawing Office and the girls of the tracing office.

With the glass roof, the building got very hot in summer and the girls of the tracing office wore as little as possible and at times seemed to deliberately offer glimpses, to boys like me, of parts of the upper female body which I had only previously seen in pictures.

A week or so before Christmas I was allowed to present, to all the staff, a list for them to contribute to my Christmas box. I remember the first time I got the huge sum of £2 9s, which I took home to my mother who allowed me to keep it and use it to buy a suit at the 'Weaver to Wearer' tailors in Newcastle, for the grand sum of £1 9s. I was proud as a peacock.

Early in 1932 I was given a list of the names of all the Drawing Office staff and was told to tell each one in turn to go to the office of Mr Kevney where they were told that they were to suffer a ten per cent cut in salary. When it came to my turn, he asked me what my wage was and when I said seven shillings and sixpence he said that I could not suffer a ten per cent cut, so I was the only one who survived the 'The Cuts'. Every winter from starting work I went to evening classes to study for an HNC. It was hard work and meant long days in the winter from 8am to 10pm three days a week.

When I was 16 I became an apprentice in the Engineering Works and had to start at 7.30 am and worked until 5pm with one hour for lunch. And we also worked a Saturday morning 7.30 am until 12 noon. Evening classes had to be attended and I also played rugby for Vickers-Armstrongs 3rd team.

My first job as a 16-year-old was in the Assembly Shop under Mr Wylie, a strict man, always in a white coat and a black bowler hat. I was the junior in a group of five fitters headed by an elderly man called Jack Cooke, with a lot of patience to teach me how to become a skilled fitter. Our team had the job of assembling cylinder heads for five cylinder 500 HP diesel engines used for driving oil pumps in the Middle East.

After six months of this work I was sent for by the Apprentice Supervisor who told me that I was being transferred to the Marine Engine Shop. Because my evening class results were so good, I had been selected, along with another apprentice, to spend five months each year for three years at Rutherford Technical College on a day course in Engineering.

The Marine Shop built and tested Sulzer diesel engines of 3,000 horse power for ships which carried heavy cargoes and there were large machines for turning and milling.

A skilled fitter at this time earned £2 1s per week – and they worked hard. Time keeping was strict. If an apprentice was two minutes late he lost a quarter of an hour's pay and if he lost more than two in a week he was sent home until lunchtime. At the end of his five year apprenticeship all this time was added up and he could not get a fitter's wage until he had worked that time; it was called 'Black Time'.

Any mistakes made by fitters were severely dealt with – even to being dismissed on the spot and as there was always a queue at the gate for jobs, mistakes were seldom made.

In addition to the General Engineering Shop, where I first started, there was a machine shop; all the machines being belt driven from overhead shafting, maintained by millwrights. There was also a Boiler Shop where Marine Scotch Boilers were made; a Tender Shop, building tenders for steam locomotives which were built in a shop alongside the Marine Shop. There was also a Coppersmithing Shop where all the piping for the steam locos was made and a paint shop, where the locos were

West Newcastle Local Studies

Fitters at Elswick, 1950s.

painted in the colours and livery of the Railway Company which had ordered them.

Shortly after my 19th birthday I was transferred from the workshop into the Locomotive Drawing Office as a junior draughtsman. This meant some very welcome changes in my life; I no longer had to get up at 6am in order to catch the train from Newburn at 7am after a walk of about one and a half miles from where we lived in Throckley. There were no more dirty overalls and the hours were shorter and my wage had gone up to £1 5s per week.

The Chief Draughtsman was Mr McNeil, a Scotsman, who was very strict. I worked under Mr Bob Duncan on Spencer

Hopwood Vertical Steam Boilers. He was a great help.

We had to work on a Saturday morning and were expected to wear a dark suit, white shirt and dark tie. One Saturday two of the younger draughtsmen came to work in sports jackets and Oxford Bags and when seen by Mr McNeil they were sent home as being improperly dressed.

About six months before I was 21 some of us were transferred to Vickers at Elswick as the factory at Scotswood had been turned over to Vickers management. I was put into the Hydraulic Drawing Office under Mr Bill Rutter. There were four apprentice draughtsmen, myself, Jack Anderson, Cyril Nixon and Harry Wardle.

When I was 21 my wage went up from £1 9s 6d to the princely sum of £2 10s per week.

Harry Hall

A HOT AND DANGEROUS JOB

In November 1939, two months before I was 16, I had an interview with the apprentice supervisor with the view to becoming an apprentice at Elswick Works.

After the interview I signed on the junior dole in Newcastle. I was given a card to apply for a job at Elswick works to become an apprentice moulder. At the interview I was told by the apprentice supervisor that if I got the job I would not be able to transfer to the fitting department.

I was selected and started work in the Brass Foundry and was put straight onto the bench to learn the trade, which was to make moulds of sand which were baked in ovens or a furnace. These moulds were passed on to tradesman moulders who used them to form larger moulds. It was a very dirty and hot job. Also there was the danger of flying hot brass when it hit cold sand. Despite the warning that I could not transfer, I tried different shop managers without success. I then made an application to become an apprentice electrician at Walker Naval Yard

(Vickers). I handed in my notice and started at the Naval Yard one month before my 16th birthday.

Bill Jeffries

'SNIFFING' – AND DOING THE 'BOMB SHOP RUN'

You couldn't start an apprenticeship until 16 years of age. Before that you would be a post boy or messenger boy – a bit of a dogsbody. I began my employment at Vickers-Armstrong's Elswick Works as a 14-year-old office boy sometime in 1942. The first job I was given was to work the lift in the head office building transporting high and low in the company from basement to coal loft and all floors in between. It was an interesting introduction to the hierarchical structure of the firm both in terms of how the various floors were furnished and populated, and also of not knowing who I would open the lift doors to, a director or a clerk, a draughtsman or a messenger, a smart secretary or a cleaner.

One of the advantages of meeting and serving such a wide cross-section of staff and employees in the lift was when it was nearing Christmas. Every office boy had a Christmas list to which those he served normally made a contribution. The lift boy served nearly everyone! Although there were always those who made excuses that they had already contributed to their own office boy's list, I actually did quite well.

After my job as lift boy, I was told that I was to go to work for the Lithography Dept. I learned a lot – how to set up type and work a simple printing machine, how to count and guillotine reams of paper, how to bind books and manuals. It was there that I had my first (and last) experience of 'sniffing'. Being the youngest and most naive member of the department, I was tricked one day by my slightly older colleague into 'smelling' a piece of mutton cloth which was used to clean the printing type and which had been soaked in carbon tetrachloride. The next thing I knew was when I saw an angry and concerned supervisor bending over me as I came to asking, 'What's the matter sonny?' I have never 'sniffed' since.

When my fellow office boys and I went each day for lunch to the Schools Canteen across Scotswood Road we would, in those wartime days, find a menu that was, to say the least, limited. We called the peas 'buckshot' and the steamed puddings 'lead hammers' but we still scoffed huge helpings with our adolescent appetites. On leaving the canteen, we would see the next day's fare chalked up on a blackboard at the door, and would, to exact our revenge at its execrable quality, amend 'Steamed Cod' to 'Steamed God' and 'Meat Rissoles' to 'Meat R ....sole'!

There was an apprentice in the toolroom, a very good rugby player who had played for an outside club. He turned out in the annual Elswick v. Scotswood match and had a storming game. Vickers' Rugby Secretary approached him and told him if he played for Vickers he would be kept on when he was 21. He need not have worried, with the approaching war and the rearmament which was taking place Vickers were hanging on to every worker possible. Tradesmen who had been unemployed for years were finding their way back.

At the age of 16 I had to leave the Head Office and go to the works to begin my apprenticeship. It had always been my ambition to become a draughtsman and to work in the Drawing Office, but this could not be done without first serving at least some part of one's apprenticeship in the workshops to gain a practical knowledge of engineering processes and skills. This of course meant starting work at 7.30am instead of 8.45am, something which I did not take kindly to being a poor riser. Worse still, it being wartime I had, like others, to work a fortnight's

West Newcastle Local Studies

The Elswick canteen c.1960s. WNLS.

nightshift after a fortnight's dayshift. This I detested thoroughly, but tried to keep my long term ambition in view.

In order to achieve this ambition I attended evening classes, and day-release classes at Rutherford Technical College in Bath Lane, achieving eventually both Ordinary and Higher National Certificates in Mechanical Engineering.

The department I was assigned to was the VSG Dept. VSG stood for Variable Speed Gear and was concerned with the manufacture of hydraulic pumps and motors used in various kinds of military, naval and commercial applications. My first shop was No. 131, making small units for use in aircraft. This shop was quite small compared with others. During the fortnight's nightshifts I used to go to evening classes two nights a week from 7pm till 9pm then straight to work for 9.30pm finishing at 7.30 am next morning. Saturday afternoons were also spent at classes. What a life for a 16-year-old! Other nights before going to work were spent doing homework. I only had any entertainment on a Saturday evening and on Sunday when I went to church where there was a good crowd of young people and a flourishing youth club.

Whilst working the nightshift in 131 Shop, the apprentices were allowed an extra meal break. There was no provision made for us in the way of hot water for our tea. So we had to make what was known as 'The Bomb Shop Run'. This was to the shop where bombs were made for our gallant airmen to deliver to Nazi Germany, and hot water was available – but not for anyone other than those working in that shop. Therefore each of us in turn had to run the gauntlet of Bomb Shop personnel and management, quickly fill all the cans with boiling water, and return unscathed to 131 Shop. For the most part this could be done successfully by hiding behind machinery, packing crates and piping but there was a final part of the run where you were totally exposed. Being caught meant a severe reprimand and being suspended for three days and loss of pay. Although we often wondered who was at greater risk – our bombers over Germany, or us going on 'The Bomb Shop Run', no one was ever caught to my knowledge. Getting into hot water however took on a whole new meaning for me after that experience.

As the war came to an end so did aircraft production so 131 Shop ceased to function. So, after one of my periods of day release to Rutherford, I was told to report to the main VSG Shop No. 21. This was where the bulk of hydraulic pump and motor production took place. I spent some time on the marking-off tables there and some time on the small lathes. These were sited in a gallery which ran right round the shop about half way up its walls. Below the galleries were stores for raw material and in the centre of the shop on the ground floor were the very heavy machine tools including borers and large lathes. One of these was operated by an older craftsman, by the name of Davie, who, one day, forgot to tighten the bolts holding the workpiece to the machine's faceplate. Imagine everyone's consternation when, after starting his machine, the workpiece, weighing about a ton, was flung up through the workshop roof in an arc, descending via the floor of one of the galleries and landing in the bar store on the ground level. Miraculously it didn't touch a single soul. Davie and all those around that day were suitably chastened by the experience and vowed to lead decent lives thereafter.

John Tones

ANOTHER 131 SHOP APPRENTICE
My first pair of long pants were bought when I started work at Vickers when I was 14. I was interviewed by Captain Gillman and was asked, among other things, if I played rugby or football. Although I didn't, I got the job. Work was very easy to find in 1941.

I started in 131 Shop inspection cage going messages for all the inspectors, getting drawings, making tea, going to the canteen to order meals, getting inspection gear from the store, in fact being a general dogsbody but getting to know the layout of the works fairly well. I also got to know the product of 131 shop. This was the VSG aero unit which powered the undercarriage and operated the gun turrets on RAF aircraft.

The working week was five-and-a-half days and we had to clock on for 7.30, then collect 'dummy' clocking-in cards between 12 and 1.00pm and hand these in when we finished, usually at 5 o'clock or 7.30 pm if working overtime.

My starting pay was £1 11s 3d. Any time lost (clocking in two minutes late meant that you lost a full quarter of an hour) was deducted from your pay. When I started, cash was deducted from your pay towards your one week's holiday pay – this was usually Race Week. Later we got paid for holidays. The job included making the tea for all the people in the cage (it was an inspection cage). Young lads were often sent to the store to ask for a 'long stand' or things like 'wire netting oil cans'.

I started my apprenticeship in 131 Shop in 1944 and was allocated to a fitter (there was no apprentice training school as there was later on). As all the work on the fitting bench was 'timed' the work I did was tied in somehow (I don't know quite how) with the fitter who was teaching me so that he got extra money. The work was mainly rectifying VSG pumps that had been on test beds and had failed calibration tests or needed other work doing to them.

I joined the Vickers Armstrong Apprentices' Welfare Club which was on the north side of Scotswood Road.

West Newcastle Local Studies

Apprentices at Elswick Works, c.1950s with the parts of a model clearing press laid out.

This cost twopence a week which was deducted from your wages and for this you had the use of snooker tables, boxing rings and gymnastic gear and training was given. We also had use of a very extensive library. I also joined the Sports Club which was just off Ferguson Lane. There there were large playing fields – football and rugby pitches, cricket pitches, bowling greens, changing rooms and a club house where drinks could be bought. Vickers held the annual Sports Day here.

After a while I was put into the test room where various tests were done to make sure the pumps were doing what they were meant to do. Most of the staff there were women who car-

ried out the tests while we set up the test beds. There were a lot of ladies employed during the war doing long shifts and working at night as well. I did night shifts as well and the most bizarre thing about it was eating Vienna steak and chips at 2.30 am.

In September 1945 I was transferred to 21 Shop VSG where much larger VSG Units were made for warships and there was one spare unit for the battleship *King George V* which was never used. In 1947 I asked for, and got, a transfer to Vickers garage. I think I learned more in the garage about fitting and turning than I did in the VSG because we had to do all our own

A football match against Barrow c.1960. Being good at football was a great help to the young apprentice.

It was certainly a shock to the system to start life in a factory. I began life in 27 Shop plan store as a plan lad for the princely sum of £2 7s 6d per week, and that was for long hours in those days. I can't recall, exactly, what the hours were, but they seemed to be an eternity at the time.

I can remember the overpowering smell of cutting oil in the air. Nobody knew or seemed to care what it could do to your health in those days.

After my 16th birthday, I was sent to the Apprentice Training School, which was run along very strict lines – probably necessary with some of the apprentices. I recall one of the most productive jobs done in the Training School was to produce discs (without the knowledge of the training officers) which worked very well in the tobacco machines at the local shops, until they were discovered following complaints from the shopkeepers. Some also plied a lucrative trade pinching brass to sell at the local scrap yards, with no questions asked. We did receive some training while all this was going on.

The apprentices were asked what trade they wished to follow but it nearly always turned out to be a fitter or turner. My ambitions took another route when the fabrication shop advertised for metal workers, which meant leaving the Training School and working in 50 Shop and, after an interview with one of the old foremen, I got the job. I think they would have taken the factory cat, if it had applied, and you found out why when

machining, the variety of trucks and private cars was enormous and the men there were great instructors. I ended my apprenticeship there in 1949.

William Bell

A SHOCK TO THE SYSTEM

I left school at 15 to join Vickers-Armstrongs Elswick works. In those days, around 1962, the best chance of an apprenticeship was a family history at the works with someone to recommend you. In my case my father worked at the site along with two uncles and previously a grandfather and a great grandfather. This carried more sway than qualifications in those days. The ability to play football also helped. Apprenticeships were more for those who left school without exam passes. The Grammar School educated people went into office work in the main.

you saw the working conditions in those days.

Vickers-Armstrongs had a reputation in those days for turning out the finest apprentices in the country, but we received a sub-standard apprenticeship. Nobody cared if we had a planned and structured training programme, as they have now. We were on piece work from day one and all we produced were minor details, such as cable clips, working under the stare of the supervisor. We felt we were just cheap labour. Those who were lucky enough to work with a tradesman at least had the chance to learn from him, even though the main task was to help him make

Apprentices outside the Apprentice Training School, Elswick, February 1982.

a bonus. I had to leave Vickers to learn my trade, and this I did as soon as I was 21.

I had my first encounter with the trade unions in those days. I joined the Sheetmetal Workers Union when I was 16 to see the metalworkers go out on strike nearly every Monday afternoon. This was the result of an agreement that if time for a piece price was not settled by the Monday, the men walked out on strike in support of the man in dispute. Unfortunately we apprentices were not allowed to join them. I suspect the real reason for the strikes was an afternoon in the pub. I remember

the manager of the fabrication department said he was becoming the joke of the boardroom and was frequently asked if they were 'in' or 'out' over lunch. I remember many a person throwing their tea and sandwiches under the table at the sight of one the managers, who would sack anyone caught drinking tea in works time.

T.A.M. Spence

Wartime Workers

The Second World War brought bombing to all major centres of population, including Tyneside. One hundred and forty-one people were killed and 587 injured in Newcastle during the conflict. The New Bridge Street Goods Station was bombed on the night of 1 September 1941 and blazed for two days. Vickers-Armstrongs' production for the war effort was phenomenal including: 33,000 guns and gun barrels, 860 naval gun mountings, 3,500 gun carriages, a million and a quarter shells and bombs, 11 million cartridge cases, 16 million fuses, 23,000 aircraft undercarriages, 3,500 tanks. New workers were taken on, many of them women.

MODERNISING THE FACTORY – THE BUILD-UP TO WAR, 1934

I would say this was about the time things started moving. Every department had an increase in employment. We, the plumbers and steelworkers, were moved into 39A Shop so that they could be prepared for building war ships. The first was 29 Shop but the old one had to be demolished first of all.

This job fascinated me, they didn't have the equipment that is available now but they bashed on regardless. After removing all machines in the two south bays we went in and removed all pipe-work and made things safe. Other squads went in and took down the belt-drive shafts. They dropped a tarpaulin screen down the centre of the shop so that the other boys could still carry on working.

The builders and navvies were called in to strip the roof and as there were no cranes the navvies had to saw the trusses at each end and let them fall to the floor to be dismantled. There was another team of engine-drivers, steam-crane drivers and plate-layers. If it had not been for them the factory would have been at a standstill. They were the only means of transport. Everything came and went by rail and there weren't many shops that didn't have a line laid to them.

After clearing the roof they brought the steam crane into operation. The rail line was about ten feet from the front of the building, so they attached a heavy steel ball to the hook of the crane and knocked down the wall, leaving the cast-iron columns. Then they attached a hawser to the engine and the columns to snap them off at low level, for digging out.

The new girders, columns and trusses were brought from outside. After clearing the floor the platelayers laid a temporary track up the centre of each bay, so that after putting a short extension on the jib of the crane they could start putting up the new shop. Once started, the plumbers took sizes and made templates of the gutters. We had to make brackets to carry them. The crane also came in very handy. Once they got the girders up we used the brackets so that we could lay the gutters in and the crane lifted them for us. There was a stone put on the end of the building dated 1935.

There were wagon loads of 4 inch diameter pipes from the railways sidings. We had to unload them and store them in one of the old shops. A new plumber started and I was sent with him to put a triple run of pipes down each bay, leaving a walkway between the two middle columns, then fit a steam pipe as a heating system. As the steam came I think it pleased the machine-men as they had never been used to it. Some chaps had small ovens made to hang on the pipes and warm their pies

Elswick Works, 1949. The works stretched down the Tyne from Benwell to Water Street in the foreground. The works is gone now, and Armstrong Business park occupies the site.

for lunch. A chap was telling me that one or two brought young plants in to bring them on.

The manager, Mr Muirhead, had an office built alongside a medical centre with an office for a doctor. The floor above was made into a saddler's shop where they made padding for the tank seats. It was said that Mr Muirhead was a stickler for perfection. Every morning when coming for work he walked through the rows of machines and if anything was out of place he laid the law down.

G. Carr

The underpass from Scotswood Road to Elswick works and main offices, April 1969.

WARTIME WORK AT SCOTSWOOD

By devious methods I was able to leave Elswick tool room and restart as a toolmaker at the Scotswood works. Vickers had taken over Scotswood works in 1937, and Armstrong's factory was no more. The last locomotive had been completed, and the large spacious shops were laid out for gun production and armament manufacture. The layout of the factory compared to the rambling Elswick works was infinitely better. Shops 3 or 4 which had been locomotive tender shops were probably over 200 yards long. These shops were ideally suited for gun production. Anti aircraft guns 3.7, 4.5 and 5.5, Howitzers 3.45 (25 pounders) 2 pounders were all made in these shops. Breech blocks and jackets were also manufactured.

After Dunkirk the production was phenomenal. As many as 600 men were employed in these shops. I was part of a team of eight toolmakers who made the tools and gauges. The tooling for this production was extremely hard to keep up with. The graph of production seemed to go up each week until 1944 The large machine shop, 15, was a multi products shop, housing the main tool room. Pedestal naval deck pom poms were made there (Chicago Pianos they were called). The Dam Buster bombs were made in this shop. The big machine section was always referred to as the Park – apparently in the First War shells were filled with cordite, and it had the detrimental effect of turning employees' hair and skin green. The antidote for this was to place plants in the workshop. 15 Shop was referred to as the Park for the next 40 years!

The other end of the factory 'east', which the old hands referred to as 'the Saurer end', was where Armstrong Saurer Diesel lorries had been made. During the war Olio legs were made here for RAF

24

planes' retractable undercarriages. This area of the works is now the Michel Bearings section of the Vickers group. As the war situation improved, production slowed down, and by early 1945 some of the employees were being allowed to leave.

Alan Evans

ALONG SCOTSWOOD ROAD

Starting from the boundary on Scotswood Road, there were four buildings – two pattern stores, the staff canteen and the Admiralty Building. The first store held a massive gas meter, next there was a sprinkler system, then the entrance to the brass foundry with the office on your left, and a staircase. There was another staircase to the basement. All the floors were full of racks, carrying patterns of all descriptions, I think for the brass foundry. As employment picked up there were more men started and they had a fair way to walk for meals so they decided to clear part of the first floor and put in a kitchen and dining room.

The other pattern store was much bigger – full of patterns – except one end of the second floor was cleared for joiners to make mock-ups of different jobs they intended to build. The next building was the staff canteen, but I think with war being imminent, and having a large intake of new employees, there wasn't room at the school canteen, so they made it suitable for the overspill. Next came the gate-keeper's lodge, and as the staff had to cross the railway lines, he had to look after the gate and see it was safe for them to cross. Then came the Admiralty Building – I can't say what happened there. I know there were quite a few

offices, but when I used to go in to do a repair, I never noticed much activity.

The subway entrance came next. You had to go down hill, as you had to go under the railway. There was also a stairway which brought you back onto Scotswood Road. From the roadway there was another stairway that took you to a bridge over the railway which led to the entrance to the main store. At the end of the store the bridge from Elswick pit brought the coals down to the jetty.

G. Carr

GOOD TIMES, BAD TIMES – AND NO HEATING

During the war we were earning good money and there was always plenty of work. There was an *esprit de corps*, a bit of fun going on. There was a feeling of danger. Everyone knew some-

Women at lathes in 39c Shop, Elswick, c.1940.

25

one who was killed or injured. At the beginning of the war, every night for eight months, German planes flew over the works driving people into shelters and stopping production. But there was nothing to spend your money on, no food, no clothes and no holidays. Your formative years were being wasted. Yes, there were dances and pictures and pubs but we were either working or were too tired to go out.

There were long hours – 12 hour shifts for 14 days then a 24 hour break. There were day shifts and night shifts. In fact the factory was working round the clock. People couldn't get off for night school. There was some day-release awarded for technical school studies but only for the star pupils. A lot of people on munitions wanted to join the forces. It seemed an easier life than 12 hours and seven days. There was the glamour of the uniform – attracting girls at dances. Lots of men over 18 in reserved occupations felt that they should be out there fighting like their brothers or friends. Factory conditions were dreadful – there was only one heating brazier in the middle of each shop.

The Ministry of Defence moved labour in and out of factories and dilutees [people brought in to increase the workforce] were allowed into the factories, after training. Though semi-skilled people existed before the war, this was extended by dilutees, including women. At the end of the war skill demarcation was reinforced and most women and dilutees were dismissed.

A lot of very sophisticated machines were imported from the USA. These were well in advance of Vickers' equipment and this really was the start of building the quality into the machine – rather than relying on the traditional skill of the operator.

Fifty per cent of output was guns, 33 per cent was tanks. Aircraft – Spitfires and Wellingtons – and ships were made too. People worked hard. They were nervous of being conquered by the Germans but were very uplifted by Churchill who was on the wireless encouraging the British people. He spoke of his concerns but also about his tremendous confidence in victory.

There were regular ENSA concerts and speeches from serving officers in the canteen at lunchtime.

There was certainly a lack of food. My own major memory of war was that I was always hungry. Food was basic – bread, potatoes, turnips, milk, carrots (which helped you see in the blackout!) and halibut oil tablets issued to workers with their pay, but everything else was rationed. Eggs, meat, bacon, cheese, sausages and liver were available sometimes but you had to queue for hours for them. People were encouraged to dig for victory – keeping chickens and pigs, but you couldn't slaughter them – they had to be handed over.

Beer was available but the pubs were always running out. People rushed around looking for open pubs. There were often no glasses. People were rationed to one pint of beer in some pubs. People tended to try to become known as a regular customer at several pubs.

Eddie Mullin

AIR RAID WARNINGS
There was a thing happened during the war. I think it funny now. There were fire watchers there to keep their eyes on things. There was a raid one night, an aircraft came over and dropped a stack of incendiaries. One fell on Scotswood Road, another on a pattern store, another on the rolling mill dept landed on top of a gas meter. It so happened there was a chap there and he knocked it to the floor. The one that hit the store went through the roof, burnt through a pattern, set the sprinklers off, the water flowed all the way to the basement and it was eventually put out. The fire watchers didn't know a thing about it, though it must have wakened everybody in Elswick. Consequently the two large gongs on the outside of the buildings had to be scrapped and they rigged up an electrical control to the fire station.

G.Carr

DAY AND NIGHT, NIGHT AND DAY

I'll always remember working during the war at Vickers-Armstrongs. We worked 60 hours a week, 12 hours a day. One week it was night shift the next day shift. Night shift was my worst time as my stomach was bad all the week. I only ate one meal a day that was my breakfast when I came off night shift and I only had an apple through the night.

I was gauger, testing all the shell parts as they came off the machines for any faults. It was very bad for my eyes as the metal was brass and aluminium which was very bright and you had to look into all the parts for faults. If any were found you would have to stop the machine until the fitter put it right. The fitters were all old men as all the young men were called up for service. All the machines were worked by women.

We caught a bus from Whickham at 7 o'clock, then a tram car that took us along Scotswood Road. Sometimes we would just finish work and go for the bus and the sirens would sound, so we were not allowed home until the all clear. Often that was 12 o'clock at night and as you were going home in the bus the guns from Lobley Hill would be firing and also the ones from Whickham. The windows felt as if they were being blasted in. One night coming from work the sirens went and they began to drop what were called 'Flaming Onions'. They lit up where they wanted to bomb, which on this occasion happened to be the Goods Station in Newcastle. One night I remember I was so tired after coming in from work through the night. The sirens went and my mother told me to get up. However I said no as I was too tired. If they bombed me that was it. Just then the bomb came whirling down and we all dived under the stairs. That night they dropped about three bombs in the Whickham area.

My factory was No. 2 Shop. They were all just steel

West Newcastle Local Studies

Demonstrating a mould for a shell.

Women at work in the VSG section at the end of the war.

buildings and very cold with stone floors and blacked out windows, so the big doors were kept open all day long. At night that was different as everything was blacked out and the fumes and smoke from all the machines working was unbearable – no fresh air at all. My free day on Sunday I spent trying to walk around in the fresh air for my lungs. We tried at dinner times to sign on for the Land Army or Wrens. However they told us we were too important to leave as we were making shells for the war.

Often when they tried to bomb the factory we were told to put on our tin hats and go into the shelters but there was so much shrapnel from our guns flying about we didn't bother.

When the war ended I was glad to leave for another job as all I was paid for those 60 hour weeks was £2 weekly.

Dorothy Harm

Women in 27 Shop, c.1940.

West Newcastle Local Studies

A VICKERS FAMILY

We were a Vickers family as my grandfather worked as an engineer from the late 1800s into the early 1900s when he retired at seventy. My mother worked in 40 Shop, Scotswood, during the First War with my aunt, who retired after 44 years service. She was in charge of the Lacquer Room in 39 Shop at that time. My father worked as a storekeeper, from 1935-1964, and my sister was drafted in for war work, then sent to work in Coventry through the Bevan Scheme.

I myself started at 16 years old on December 4th 1938. It was very strange having to get up in the mornings in the dark at 6.30am to start at 7.30, as I had previously been in a shop. There were six new starters that morning, and we were given overalls which came down to our feet, and caps to cover our hair (all of

it). Two of us were put on the grinding section, small machines with a sapphire stone wheel. The components for the fuse work were the same as the workings in a watch or clock.

It was very strict. There were three forewomen walking the floor, to make sure we got on with our work. We were not allowed to wear nail varnish or lipstick. Anyone caught with either was made to remove it. We worked from 7.30am to 5.15pm on a flat rate of pay, which in old money was 17 shillings and fourpence. When we finally went on to piece work, it was wonderful to make £1.

There was a glass roof in 26 Shop, which was painted black to prepare for the blackout, as the war was about to start. This meant we hardly ever saw daylight, as we had to work 12 hour shifts seven days a week. There were small red lights fitted to the roof, and when there was an air raid, which was usually

Rebecca Watson operating a pinion lathe, c.1940.

utes, I waited that snowy morning until it was daylight before I ventured forth. I remember the snow was knee high, and being one of the first to make tracks it took twice as long for the journey. After finally getting to work I was told off for being late, and lost half an hour's pay as well.

At Christmas we were allowed to decorate our section, and also about an hour off to have a party on Christmas Eve. We had the choice of the party or going home, so a few of us did that.

There were 2,000 women in Vickers which included, Elswick, Scotswood and Team Valley. The head supervisor was Mrs Stewart. She was first made a forewoman in the First War, then Personnel Officer over all of these factory shops until she retired with the British Empire Medal which I think would be 1947.

In 1945, at the end of the war, 26 Shop received a framed letter from the Governor of Malta, thanking the workforce for helping to save his island, which was a very nice compliment for everyone.

Rebecca Watson

when we were starting on our meal break, especially on night shift, we were warned by a claxon blowing – but we weren't allowed to go into the shelter, which was on the riverside, until the red lights went on. This meant that enemy aircraft were now over the Tyne.

Some of the sections were on two shifts, 6am - 2pm and 10pm - 6am. I was lucky I only did days and nights. I was told to start on night shift as soon as I was 18.

The only men in 26 Shop, were the setters for the machines, and as they were called up for the forces, some of the women were trained to take their places, and they were very good.

In 1941 we had one of the worst snow storms, and as I always had to walk to work which normally took about 30 min-

MAKING SHELLS

During the Second World War I worked at Vickers-Armstrongs helping to produce 25lb shells. My first job was operating a lathe which reduced the shell to a certain weight. I had a pair of scales for checking.

The shells were inserted into the aperture of the furnace with long metal tongs. You had to wear special gloves. The shells rotated at a very slow pace to complete the full circle (about one hour) and then they were removed from the terrific heat by the same method, and immediately transferred, nose down, into a machine that held them in a metal frame which rotated, gradually lowering only the nose of the shell to be submerged in water. This was part of the hardening process.

While working on this we had to attend the first aid room a certain number of times during our working hours to drink a specified measure of salt water to replace the salt our bodies lost because of the intense heat. I must say it was quite horrible and we did our best to avoid it, but the nurse kept a watchful eye on us.

In 1943 what was called a 'circular hearth', which had been constructed somewhere in Scotland, was brought to the factory. It was delivered on a Sunday (when roads were most quiet) under police escort to clear the forward route. It was quite a dangerous undertaking because of its enormous size. This hearth of course abolished the use of the old furnace method.

Vickers

Giant gunpits were sunk at the Elswick works during the war.

We worked very, very hard and gained the admiration of our manager Jack Douglas who was very doubtful about how he could cope with a bevy of girls, having always worked with men. He was a great fellow who unfortunately had to have a leg amputated due to an accident at work. I was so sad to hear of this.

The girls in this shop came from all walks of life – a professional dancer, a singer with Joe Loss's dance band, secretaries, shop assistants, to name but a few – but what comradeship and friendships made to last all these years! In the beginning we were not allowed to smoke in the factory so we had to sneak away to the loo for a fag, but after we joined a union they got the ban lifted.

Pat Marvell

The Post-War Boom

A description in the Tyneside Official Industrial Handbook published during the 1950s reads: 'At Elswick and Scotswood on the Tyne, are two of the works of Vickers-Armstrongs; 125 acres of engineering shops, machine shops and foundries. For the second time in a generation, these works have undertaken and completed the reorganisation imposed by the change from war to peace. Now they are busy again on a peace footing … The world still stands in great need of what Elswick and Scotswood have to give – men, machines and workmanship representing an enormous production potential… great technical skill and immense resources are helping to restore production in the post-war world.'

A Shervick tractor, converted from a Sherman tank c.1950.

PLENTY OF WORK

This was an exciting time. The war had been won. The forces were gradually being demobbed. As very few Vickers workers had been conscripted because it was a reserved occupation, little reorganisation took place in the works – though people in their late sixties and early seventies were retiring (there was no fixed retirement age of 65 in those days). Some women employed in the factories were being finished and some of the workers were taken into the forces for two years. There was loads of work, loads of overtime, and no fear of bombing.

Vickers was booming. The shipyards were replacing

destroyed vessels – and there was growth in commercial aircraft. Efforts were being made to get into non-armament work. Shervick tractors (based on the Sherman tank) – were trialled on the Government Scheme. Vickers also went into printing, office equipment, packaging, instruments, medical, chemical, engineering, buying out existing companies, making products that would fit in with the plant and worker skills.

Vickers started moving products about. The Variable Speed Gear (VSG) went to Weymouth and Gun Mountings went to Vickers Barrow works. However, on Tyneside there was great confidence. There was plenty of work. The Unions were strong and the men were highly paid for good engineering skills – Elswick had the highest pay rates in the district.

Eddie Mullin

West Newcastle Local Studies

After World War II trains were reconditioned at Scotswood works. This photograph was taken in 1946 and shows the Ord Arms and Wheelers dance hall on Scotswood Road. The clock tower now stands on Scottish & Newcastle Breweries in Bath Lane, Newcastle.

THE ELECTRICAL INSPECTOR
In 1956 I applied to be an electrical inspector at Vickers Elswick, where I worked on various types of military tanks, examining and testing all installations. I also tested incoming goods. Gun control checks were done outside the workshops. A certain number of tanks had to be tested on the moors at Ridsdale,

where the vehicle was driven over a track, and up and down ditches, in a figure of eight while the gunner had to be able to keep the gun on the target.

Bill Jeffries

MAKING PRESSINGS
In 1965-66 I was transferred as assistant manager to 33 Shop attached to the Die Division which then became the Pressings

Above: Gun equipment X3 prototype, July 1957. Below: Elswick rate fixers, c.1950s.

Division. As well as making Fix Bins, a large variety of pressings were produced including pressing out large ball-race brass rings from solid bars. The hydraulic presses used were dated 1901.

William Bell

THE RATE FIXERS

The most hated men in Vickers were the rate fixers who had the ability to make a man's working life a misery by issuing poor piece work prices, which could cut a man's earnings substantially.

The rate fixing staff were in the same office as the draughtsmen and we were able to hear the arguments about the piece prices. I well remember one machine operator leaving the office after failing to get an increase on his time. He called to the rate fixers, "I believe you're moving house Bob." The rate fixer was surprised at being spoken to so civilly. He replied, "Yes, do you know the street I'm moving to?" "No," was the reply, "but I hope the former occupant leaves all the gas taps on in the house!"

Tommy Spence

Getting Away From It All – Ridsdale Firing Range

Tanks were taken up to the firing ranges on the moors at Ridsdale near Otterburn in Northumberland. They could not be tested, for obvious reasons, in the works themselves.

There was a railway link from Newcastle via Morpeth through Scots Gap and Ridsdale village to Bellingham. A branch offshoot passed through to buffers just south of the main battery. This enabled heavy guns to be transported from Vickers to the range in the Northumbrian countryside for proofing.

The travelling crane was just to the north of the branch line which meant heavy equipment could be easily offloaded from the freight railway tenders. The main battery was fixed into a box type concrete structure which was filled with sand. After one day when a 4.5 inch shell did an about turn we bought an ex-government surplus mine detector which was used to detect the solid shells.

There was also a cross-battery which was situated behind the crane and fired over the railway line. This battery was used to test low-calibre weapons like machine guns but with the post-war advances in technology it was rarely used. The only occasion I can remember it ever being used was to evaluate the performance of a 0.5 inch recoil-less gun

which was to be fitted to fighter aircraft but was overtaken by the rapid development of the guided missile. The idea behind the recoil-less gun was to eliminate the 90mph speed drop

West Newcastle Local Studies (Jimmy Forsyth)

A tank proceeds down Gloucester Street, c.1955. The vibrations could ruin the beer in the barrels at the Gloucester Arms.

A tank is put through its paces on the moors at Ridsdale.

route to Ridsdale. The safety precautions were first class, the tank being preceded by a van carrying a warning sign: 'Wide Heavy Load Following' and in addition a following van had a similar sign. Many a representative in a hurry to attend a meeting came down the A68 over the top of a rise to be confronted with a 105mm gun pointing straight at him (a good road-rage deterrent).

One other thing, which was carried out at the request of the public, was to ensure that the tank exhausts were fitted to point upwards. This was to ensure that the skirts of the ladies on the West Road did not rise to shoulder height. Rubber pads were also fitted to the vehicle tracks to avoid damage to the public highway and a consequent bill from the Northumberland County Council.

At the entrance to the Range House mess there were two miniature cannon and if, before lunch, a very successful shoot had been carried out both the cannon were fully elevated. If no results had been obtained both were fully depressed and any other performance resulted in an intermediate setting.

I must admit that I was rather surprised to find 12 number 12.5 inch guns at Ridsdale which had been ordered by the Turks to defend the Dardanelles before 1914 but had not been delivered. It was rather amazing that they had remained untouched for over 40 years while householders and schools were being robbed of their railings.

Bill Wilson

which occurred when a fighter fired off all its armament.

The overhead crane was very noisy and considerable difficulty was experienced in making the crane driver understand the required movements. In an effort to overcome this, it was suggested that the points of the compass be painted on the crane structure. Unfortunately at the first attempt N, S, E and W were painted on one of the gear wheels which created even more confusion!

The range was also used to evaluate the performance of tanks. The vehicles travelled by road from Elswick and with a halt at the Tone Inn, a check was done for any system leaks. The vehicles then proceeded to the range and on arrival the fuel system was topped up and the amount of fuel was recorded.

During the Korean war, vehicles were frequently seen *en*

Life in the Drawing Office

The Drawing Office was a place to aspire to, and had an atmosphere all of its own.

DRAWING OFFICE WORK

The work of the Drawing Office is first to design the product and then to produce drawings for production.

The drawing office itself has been vastly updated since years ago. Originally a draughtsman used a drawing board, tee square, set squares and compasses. This progressed to draughting machines and finally to computers which have made the production of drawings much simpler and quicker.

Jack Daglish

HAPPY MEMORIES

There are plenty of happy memories of the Drawing Office. For instance we used to lower a tin with money for the ice-cream vendor at the foot of Water Street. And there was the demonstration of Christmas toys bought by colleagues for their young children which was interrupted when the chief draughtsman entered and found things running about his feet – within seconds everyone was back at their drawing boards and working as normal. It was a hard-working group and above all a very, very happy atmosphere. Eventually the Tank Drawing Office was moved to Head Office at Scotswood.

W.R.N. Armstrong

Drawing Office staff c.1950.

THE VSG DRAWING OFFICE

I started at Vickers Armstrong in 1955 and found myself in the VSG drawing office. The VSG units were hydraulic pumps and motors which were used in systems and processors where a fine and stepless speed control was required: steel mills, ships' steering gear, stabilisers and conveyor belts.

The drawing office was divided into two main sections, design and commercial. The commercial section, in which I worked, was itself divided into two in the charge of two section leaders who worked under the chief draughtsman.

The office was rather dirty despite the efforts of the cleaner who sucked up the dust every night using a vacuum system built into the floor. This was because the whole Scotswood area served as a dust drain for the rest of Newcastle, and with a strong west or east wind walking along the Scotswood road was like experiencing a desert sandstorm. The desks in the drawing office had quite a coating of black muck in the mornings. The furniture was very old and we worked sitting on stools, slumped over huge, slightly tilted drawing boards with five-foot long tee-squares. All other drawing equipment, except pencils and paper, had to be supplied by the draughtsman himself

There were about 16 draughtsmen, two tracers (ladies), five schedule clerks and three other clerks in the commercial section. The tracers prepared drawings when special presentation was required. They did this by overlaying a print of a drawing with a transparent sheet and tracing over the draughtsman's lines in Indian Ink and rewriting all text and figures using stencils. The result was a clear, well finished, drawing with all lines of a uniform thickness and printing of uniform size. However the drawings thus rendered lost all character and style – much as computer generated drawings today.

The schedule clerks drew up lists of parts required for customers' orders and worked closely with the draughtsmen. I found that there was not a lot of original work among the draughtsmen: mostly we were slightly modifying existing drawings for special

West Newcastle Local Studies

The Tracing Office, c.1950.

requirements or making an existing design longer or shorter or whatever. We would often relieve the tedium by recasting a design on our own initiative to make it more economical or accessible.

Occasionally we would get an original enquiry. The draughtsman would be handed a file of letters and information and told to get on with it. The draughtsman would then draw up proposals, write to customers and generally handle the job as if he were an autonomous company. However, all correspondence went through the general office and these people made sure that the draughtsman had no inkling of prices or charges. The letter files held a mass of black splodges where they had been erased, and I remember that we all somewhat resented this treatment.

West Newcastle Local Studies

Elswick Print Room: filling in drawings.

The ADO (Armament Drawing Office) was divided into about five different offices but I had dealings with only two of these: ADO1 and ADO4. ADO1 was some distance from the VSG and was a vast barn of a place – very much like an aircraft hangar. It was very spacious and airy but a bit cold-looking and uninteresting and must have contained more than a hundred people. ADO4 was much small-er and more friendly. These people worked on ships' guided missile systems and they all seemed to work steadily enough and there was no hint of warning of any kind of how their behaviour would change in the approach to Christmas.

One day just before Christmas, one of my colleagues suggested that I should take a look at the goings on in the ADO. I was absolutely astonished by what I saw. All the benches in the place were covered by structures, mainly of card and paper. These were ingenious working models of various kinds, tableaux, pictures and all sorts of things. There were great lines of streamers overhead. I saw MERRY CHRISTMAS in foot-high letters in bold relief which had been ingeniously made from empty Woodbine packets, high up on the wall. In the benches near the centre were two railway layouts. One was a sort of ghost-train idea in which the toy train crashed through cardboard swing doors and into a long tunnel and round again. On its way the train would knock against trip levers which caused little doors to open and expose skeletons and the like. There was an 'anti-gravity' machine. This was a structure which held up a spiral of cardboard tubes with little flashlight bulbs at intervals. When a steel ball was fed in at the bottom, after a second or two the lowest light flashed and the next highest and so on up to the top. What really happened, of course, was that a hidden ball was released at the top and ran down, but the bulbs were wired up to give the opposite impression. A model of Vickers main entrance stood on one bench and across a gangway was a model of the Moulder's Arms, a pub on the other side of Scotswood Road, and aerial ropes connecting the two with little cars shunting back and forth continually. The whole place was chock full of similar pieces and it took a good hour to go round and appreciate them all.

Every year, for about four or five weeks, the place was given over to this kind of activity and was one of the most amazing things I ever saw at work. In the year of the Sputnik (1957), besides the usual stuff there were about 50 of these satellites hanging from the ceiling. Part of this particular enthusiasm for Russian space travel was due to the socialist leanings of most of the staff.

Each year the draughtsmen would strive to be more original and more ingenious than before. The displays were all scrapped and thrown away between Christmas and New Year and all was earnest normality until late November again. In the VSG, by contrast, there was never so much as a robin. One year the ADO sent us a cardboard coffin labelled 'the spirit of Christmas'.

The main business of Vickers Ltd was armaments and its main paymaster was the government, through the Admiralty and the War Office. The system of payment, for whatever reason, was what was called 'cost-plus'. By this system Vickers would declare their costs on a contract, subject to inspections, and the government would meet these plus a guaranteed profit to the firm. Naturally, such a system, even among the most well intentioned of people (and I think Vickers Ltd, both management and staff, was largely well intentioned) is open to abuse which may creep in in a small but increasingly habitual way.

Many of the staff kept their wages secret and every year would make an appointment with the boss and argue their case for getting a rise, citing what jobs they had done, their level of responsibility and so on. Sometimes they were lucky and came away with ten bob or a pound a week rise. It did give rise to jealousies and ingenious attempts to find out what the other man was getting and was all faintly unsavoury.

Eric Shields

Workers' Playtime

About 1924 the company, then Armstrong, Whitworth, purchased a new ground of some 15 acres at Ferguson's Lane, Benwell. The ground catered for employees from both the Elswick and Scotswood Works, so there was no shortage of members for various sports which took place on the ground.

VICKERS-ARMSTRONGS' SPORTS CLUB

Every outdoor sport was catered for, rugby, cricket, football, hockey, tennis and later bowls. The rugby section ran three 15s, the cricket three 11s, there was one senior football team and two apprentice football teams. The tennis section had about ten courts, both hard and grass.

All members who played for the various sections were required to be members of the Sports Club and a small weekly deduction was taken from wages. There was also an additional deduction from members for their respective sports. The apprentices had to be members of the Apprentices Welfare Club, which allowed them to play for the football teams, and also to attend the Club Institute where they had boxing, gymnastics, and a billiard room.

The senior football side played in the Northern Amateur League, which … was of very high standard. The apprentices' team 18-21 played in the Welfare League. The teams were from all the major engineering firms on Tyneside, again it was of very high standard. Many of these lads could have gone to profes-

West Newcastle Local Studies

Football at Benwell Sports Ground c.1950.

Sports day, c.1950 at Benwell Sports ground.

the employees, and also open competitions which attracted some of the best athletes in the area. Sometimes the club was allotted a county championship, and in the 1930s it was either a 220 yards, or 440 yards championship of Northumberland and Durham.

One of the showpieces at the Annual Sports Day was the performance by the apprentices' gymnastic team. This talented team of gymnasts was always well booked throughout the summer, appearing at sports meetings, flower shows and garden fetes.

The Vickers Cricket Team under the captaincy of Alfie Bell won the Tyneside Senior League in 1963. The Cricket Club were involved in a triangular tournament played between the three west end clubs, Vickers, Benwell, in the village, and Benwell Hill at Denton Bank, barely a cricket throw between all three clubs.

sional clubs, but the security of an apprenticeship and a job was a big inducement to remain playing for Vickers. The 16-18 team, always referred to as 'The Nippers', was a very good side and won the local junior leagues regularly.

There were inter-departmental knockout competitions in both football and cricket sections. The early rounds of the competition were quite amusing, some of the shops teams consisting of 'used to wassers' and 'never wassers'. The finals of these competitions were of very high standard, and attended by a large crowd.

The annual sports day was also a big event, with events for

Towards the end of the 60s with the dwindling number of employees at both factories it was becoming increasingly difficult to raise sides and many outsiders were recruited into the teams. The company felt it could not go on subsidising the upkeep of the ground and running of the sports club with so few members. Sadly in 1969 it was decided to sell the ground to Newcastle United Football Club for a training ground at a price of £50,000. Alas Vickers Sports Club was no more.

Alan Evans

SOCIAL LIFE

The canteen in which we draughtsmen ate was set with little tables with places for four. However, there was one corner of the room partitioned off with metal framing and frosted glass where the tables were spread with table cloths, water jugs and glasses. In this place sat the section leaders and, I think, senior clerks of similar rank.

The biggest canteen was somewhat inconveniently situated on the other side of Scotswood Road and this was where the shopfloor workers were fed. In here there were long, bare trestle tables and forms to sit on, but I found the food was all right on the few occasions I ate there.

I believe that there were, at least, three echelons above the ones that I have mentioned, catering for successively higher seniorities of staff, culminating in the Directors' Mess which had its own kitchen and serving staff. The top management contained many ex-navy types – commanders, captains, etc. and seemed to us to be very much of an Old Boys' Club.

Vickers provided a free lending library which was next to the main entrance to the main canteen on the other side of Scotswood Road. It contained many thousands of books. It was very widely used and it seemed that a bigger proportion of the shopfloor workers used the library than other staff.

One aspect of the library service I found puzzling. Each book that was lent was given a paper cover at the issue desk and this was very sensible considering the oily hands of the workers. What was odd, however, was the fact that these jackets had been made for extremely intellectual books and so you could see a dirty-handed labourer carrying away a book which

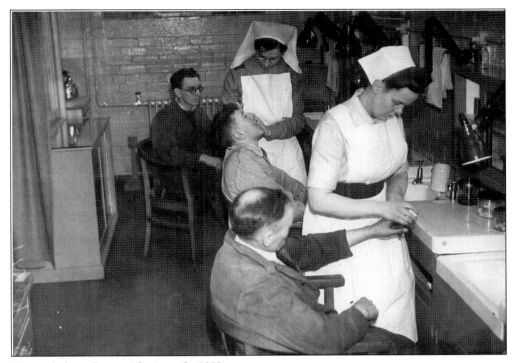

The Ambulance Room at Scotswood c.1950.

purported to be 'Essays on Neo Platonism' or something, but the labourer would sit down to enjoy 'Gunsmoke at the Lazy Y' by Zane Grey!

The Medical Room was a well-appointed place which included some expensive physiotherapy equipment and physiotherapists to match. The doctor in charge was known to be fond of doing minor surgery. He operated on me when I had a septic finger, having me anaesthetise myself with a gas-and-air machine similar to those used in childbirth.

Eric Shields

Vickers in Trouble

*V**ickers was in trouble. Its bankers began demanding changes. Over 50 per cent of the company had been lost when nationalisation of shipbuilding and aircraft had taken place in 1967.*

THE LAST ONES LEFT

A top USA consultant, McInsey, was brought in and he recommended that the company should diversify and not remain dependent on armaments. He also recommended that it divisionalise – making up smaller businesses within it, each with its own managing director responsible to head office for profitability and with its own operating plan.

This resulted in work being moved out of Elswick to other works; though Scotswood, which was the commercial Engineering Division, built cranes, power presses, STC and marine equipment. However even after McInsey, Vickers was still unable to compete for commercial work.

On Tyneside we had ordinary universal machines and superb highly paid craftsmen but we were competing with companies who had invested in sophisticated machine tools and only needed compliant, flexible operatives who were low paid. Strong trades unions at Vickers would not let pay rates slip. This battle of skill versus flexibility went on for nearly 24 years. It is over now.

It was difficult for a precision engineering company with a background in military equipment and used to cost-plus contracts to compete with companies which for years had made to-price. Vickers had no local experience of sales and marketing.

Eddie Mullin

GOODBYE TO THE ELSWICK WORKS

In the Pressings Division my job title was Production Controller. Prior to making car panels,

Traditional trade: a coppersmith bending a pipe c.1950.

West Newcastle Local Studies

as the Die Division, the press tools for making the car parts were made by a very highly skilled shop of toolmakers. Upon converting from tool making to pressing out car parts, quite a few toolmakers were kept on but the majority of workers were now press operators. My job was to produce work schedules so that parts could be ready for delivery when the customers required them. I also purchased all the sheet steel required.

We were the last division to be left on the site and we witnessed the demise of the Elswick Works. Every lunchtime I walked through the workshops and took photographs of the demolition as it progressed. The Pressings Division was now moved up to a new factory which had been part of Michael Bearings – it was quite a job moving 144 inch presses and all the smaller presses and keep production going at the same time. Vickers took over Rolls Royce Cars; so as well as all the other work we had to do for Ford Motors, etc., we also pressed out parts for the 'rollers', such as the wheel discs and the famous radiator grille parts.

William Bell

THE SAME OLD CONDITIONS

I left Vickers at 21 and worked at various places before returning, in about 1978, to the Elswick works as a sheetmetal worker in 19 Shop. The working conditions were no better than they had been when I left years before – smoky, noisy and with the most disgusting toilets you could imagine. It was bitterly cold in the winter with virtually no heating and the same outdated piecework system, virtually as it was, still in place. It was common to have earning differences of £50 a week depending on whether the foreman liked you enough to give you the better timed jobs. It was as if the whole place had been in a time warp for all those years that I had been away.

I almost quit after the first two weeks back. I still do not know why I did not, even to this day. Now I am glad I didn't. It

Vickers car pressings production line c.1970.

was during this time I was elected as a shop steward for the first time at Vickers, although I had been a shop steward at other places where I had worked. The convenor of the works at the time was Jimmy Murray, a man well respected by the workers.

Tommy Spence

The New Factory – Better for Some

NO HIDING PLACES

We moved to the new site, Scotswood, in 1982. The new factory was modern, warm, ventilated and characterless. The old hands, who did not take the redundancy offered and who came to the new site, bemoaned the lack of hiding places at the new, open-plan building, but for the younger ones, the move was easier. The conditions were far superior – a warm, well lit building and with clean, modern toilets and fume extraction in the roof, that actually worked. For me, seeing the last of the Elswick site was like shaking off all the decaying past and being offered the prospect of a better working life in the future.

Tommy Spence

AND A NEW WAY OF WORKING

In 1981 when it was decided to move to a new site at Scotswood, there were only three electrical examiners and a foreman left after redundancies. The foreman was given a year's notice of redundancy and the three examiners were also given notice but that was withdrawn, and we were asked if we could transfer to become electricians as they did not want electrical inspection at the new factory.

At Elswick Works each electrician was paid on all work booked off. Now at the new Scotswood Works it was agreed that everyone would be paid the average of the group. I was transferred for payment on the average of the whole works. The conditions at the new Scotswood Works were far superior to Elswick – and noticeably cleaner. Also, with everything under the one roof you met more people which made it all the more interesting.

It was not until 1989 that a pensioners' association was formed, prompted by myself and Alma Wheeler, to provide social events for retired workers. I'm glad to say the association is flourishing!

Bill Jeffries

Vickers

The new Vickers factory, on the site of the old Scotswood Works, 1991.

A Brief Glossary

Acetylene Torch A very hot flame from a mixture of oxygen and acetylene gases. Used for welding steel parts together or cutting through thick steel.

Anglesmith A blacksmith specialising in the manipulation of steel angle bar, shaped in the form of 'L'.

Annealing A method of softening steel or relieving stress in welded components by heating them in a large furnace.

Apprentice Young person (almost exclusively male) who underwent a period of training to become a skilled man in one of various trades. He would start on his 16th birthday and continue until 21.

Battery A site for testing firing of guns at Ridsdale, Northumberland. Later used for testing tanks.

Bevan Boy During WWII boys were conscripted to work in the mines or other specific trades instead of the forces. Named after Aneurin Bevan who was Minister of Labour during war.

Blacksmith A skilled man trained to shape steel by heating it red hot and then forming it by hand on an anvil.

Black Time Time lost during an apprenticeship which had to be made up before the apprenticeship was completed.

Boilermaker A skilled man trained to manipulate steel plate especially by bending, welding and riveting.

Breech Mechanism The mechanism at the opposite end of a gun to the mouth. This closed off the end of the gun after the shell had been loaded. It also contained the mechanism for firing the shell.

Cage Term applied to spaces within the factory enclosed by wire mesh. These were used for stores and also components which were being inspected.

Capstan (Lathe) A special type of lathe in which the part was held on a rotating plate and various tools mounted on the sides of a capstan were applied in turn to produce the required shape.

Cartridge (Case) The part of a shell system containing the explosive and detonator, usually made of brass.

Castings Components made to special (often complicated) shapes by pouring molten metal into moulds.

Class money Additional pay which was given to apprentices as an encouragement to attend evening classes. The amount was based on their exam results.

Coppersmith Skilled man trained to manipulate (mainly) copper or brass tubes and sheets.

Dambuster bombs Special bombs (spherical) designed to breech the German reservoirs by the 'Dambuster' squadron

Dies Hardened steel shapes used to manufacture rods (by pulling bars through them) or forgings (by stamping them under a forge hammer). Used to avoid complicated machining operations.

Dilutees Semi-skilled operators trained to perform a limited range of tasks.

Draughtsman Skilled man who designed components and machines and drew working diagrams so that the parts could be manufactured.

Duralium A light weight strong alloy of aluminium and copper – especially used for aircraft parts.

Estimator A skilled man who estimated the cost of producing parts by examining the drawings.

Faceplate Plate on a lathe or other machine to which components were attached ready for machining to shape.

Fitter Skilled man who was specially trained to hand-finish parts and assemble them if necessary. Also responsible for making 'jigs' to hold components and 'gauges' used to examine finished components for size.

Forgings Steel components made by shaping red hot metal by dies in a forge by applying a great pressure or by a hammer.

Furnace A large oven capable of heating components up to 1000 degrees C

Fusework Assembling the timers used to delay the detonation of shells – particularly anti-aircraft shells.

Grinding Shaping components by removing surplus metal by applying a rotating grinding wheel which was made of very hard rough material. Used to produce very accurate parts with a very smooth finish.

HNC, HND Higher National Certificate or Higher National Diploma. Qualifications obtained by study at technical colleges.

Journeyman A skilled man who had completed his apprentice training.

Lathe Machine which held the component between pointed centres while it was rotated against hardened steel tools to produce the required shapes.

Lithograph A printing method used for producing booklets and drawings in quantity.

Marking off tables Large perfectly flat steel tables which were used to support components so that they could be marked to show machinists the position of holes etc. Also used when inspecting components to see if they had been correctly made.

Measured tolerance As it is impossible to make all parts exactly to drawing the operators were allowed to deviate from the correct sizes by a fixed amount either + or – (only 1000ths of an inch were allowed). This was known as the 'tolerance'.

Milling Similar to grinding but much quicker using a shaped hardened steel tool to remove metal.

Millwright Skilled man responsible for maintenance of machinery and other equipment throughout the factory.

Moulder Worker who made moulds or shapes for castings.

Olio legs Aircraft landing carriage legs – used a hydraulic damping system (similar to car shock absorbers).

Piece rate The fixed amount of money which machine operators were given for each part machined. Faster workers made more money.

Plater (a) Skilled man who worked with steel plate by bending or forming it. Usually a Boilermaker. (b) Semi-skilled man who electro-plated components with (usually) chromium metal to give a decorative or hard finish.

Pom Poms Battery of four two-pounder guns usually mounted on warships.

Pressings Parts made from thin steel plate by pressing them into shape.

Rate-fixers Skilled men who fixed 'piece-rates'.

Shop The factory had many large buildings called 'shops' which housed machines. Most shops were divided into 'bays' each with its own overhead crane.

TDO Tank Drawing office. The department where the drawings used in the manufacture of tanks and associated items were produced.

Time-served A skilled man who had successfully completed his apprenticeship.

Turner A skilled man trained especially in the use of a lathe.

VSG Variable Speed Gear. A hydraulic device which was used for transmitting rotary motion at great power. Had the advantage of instantaneous change of speed without loss of power. Used to power gun turrets and similar applications. VSG was originally a private company, VSG Ltd, which was bought up by Vickers.

Glossary compiled by Fred Millican

Workers at Elswick, c.1970.